G.L. 5.9
#73534
Pt. 2

WITHDRAWN

G.L. 5.9
#73534
Pt. 2

ROUGH & READY
LOGGERS

A. S. Gintzler

BETHANY, MISSOURI

Acknowledgments

To the loggers and their chroniclers.

First Hardcover Library Bound Edition
Published in 1998 by Fitzgerald Books
P.O. Box 505, Bethany, Missouri 64424

Copyright © 1994 by John Muir Publications
All rights reserved.
Printed in the United States of America

Library of Congress Cataloging-in-Publication Data
Gintzler, A. S.
Rough and ready loggers / A. S. Gintzler
  p.   cm.
Includes index.
ISBN 1-887238-09-3
1. Logging—United States—History—Juvenile literature. 2. Loggers—United States—History—Juvenile literature. [1. Logging. 2. Lumber and lumbering.] I. Title.
SD538.2.A1G56 1998
634.9'8'0973—dc20   97-78363
                                        CIP
                                        AC

Logo and Cover Design: Paul Perlow
Interior Design and Typography: Linda Braun
Illustrations: Chris Brigman
Printer: Burton & Mayer, Inc.
Title page photo: A logger watches as a cut tree crashes into the surrounding forest, USDA

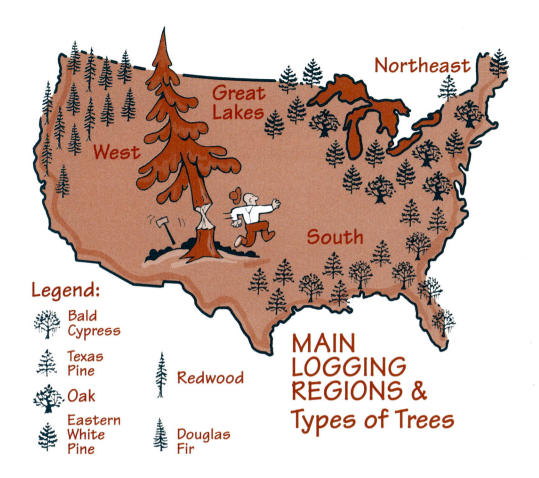

CONTENTS

The Logging Frontier 2

Indian Woodsmen 4

Pioneer Loggers 6

Logging the Northeast 8

The Log Drive 10

To the Great Lakes 12

River Rafting 14

The Lumberjack 16

The Logger's Gear 18

The Logging Camp 20

Logging Down South 22

Logging Out West 24

Logging Railroads 26

At the Sawmill 28

The Dangers of Logging 30

The Lumber Towns 32

Tall Tales and Ballads 34

Famous Loggers 36

The Lumber Barons 38

The Logger of Today 40

Logging and the Environment 42

Index 45

The Logging Frontier

Europeans who settled North America in the 1600s, 1700s, and 1800s came to a country of forests, mountains, and grasslands. Almost half of the North American continent was covered with trees.

In the East, forests stretched from the Atlantic Ocean inland for almost 1,000 miles to the Mississippi River. Forests of pine, oak, and spruce trees ran from Texas through the South for another 1,000 miles up to Maine.

Settlers in the eastern forests had never seen so many trees before. They began cutting them down to clear land for farms. The wood was used for building, heating, and tool making.

Far to the West, forests ran from Washington and Oregon south into California. Giant redwoods, fir, and spruce trees covered the Pacific coast and western mountains. Redwoods grew 250 feet tall and 15 feet wide. No European had ever seen trees so large.

Europeans had mixed feelings about so much forest. They needed the wood to build homes, but they also feared the dark, wild woodlands. For the farmer, woodlands were an enemy to be conquered. Trees covered the land he wanted to plant with crops.

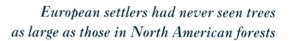

European settlers had never seen trees as large as those in North American forests

Early settlers found that North American trees and wood products were in high demand around the world. Many European countries had cut down and used up their forests long ago. England needed wood for building navy ships.

Loggers cut down trees and sold the logs. They also sawed the logs into boards, called lumber. American forests were no longer just wild woodlands that needed to be cut down to make farmlands. Wood had value. Softwood trees like pine could be made into lumber and sold for a profit.

Trees that were cut down and sold as logs or wood products were called timber. The lands where pine and other useful trees grew were called timberlands. Loggers cut timber on the first logging frontier in the Northeast until they ran out of pine. Then they moved south and west to other logging frontiers.

THE MANY USES OF WOOD

America was called a "wooden country" in the 1800s. Since forests covered much of the land, wood was used more than stone, iron, or leather. Everything from tool handles to homes and buckets to barns were made from wood. Today, wood products are even used to make paints, cardboard boxes, and paper. Giant paper mills chip wood into tiny pieces which are mixed with chemicals to make pulp and fibers which are pressed into paper.

Timber hauled out of U.S. forests was used for products around the world

By 1850, logging was the second biggest industry in the United States. Almost 56,000 loggers worked at cutting trees, moving logs, and sawing lumber. The logging industry grew as pioneers settled the continent and built towns and cities. By 1909, more than 500,000 Americans worked in the logging industry.

Logging work required special skills and a lot of muscle. The work created a new breed of American laborer called the logger, or lumberjack. Loggers lived differently than most people. They spent months and years in the deep woods, far from their homes and families.

Lumberjacks were always on the move from one logging frontier to the next. They were like cowboys, herding logs instead of cows. Lumberjacks worked for logging businessmen, called lumbermen, who owned the timberlands, the trees, and the sawmills.

Loggers, lumbermen, and most Americans were hungry for timber. But as trees came down, forests were destroyed. By 1920, almost half of America's forests were gone. Logging continued, but people began to find ways to protect, save, and restore the nation's forests.

Pilgrims began using logs for housing and tools almost as soon as they arrived

Indian Woodsmen

Before Europeans arrived in North America, forests covered much of the land—but not all of it. Woodlands opened into small and large clearings, meadows and grasslands. Much of this open land had been created on purpose by the first people of North America—the Native Americans.

Native Americans began shaping the land as early as 30,000 years ago. At that time, North American forests were first forming. Before then, much of the land had been covered by great sheets of ice called glaciers. As the climate warmed and glaciers melted, prehistoric forests began to grow.

The Native American people didn't welcome the growth of woodlands. They were hunters who depended on wild buffalo and elk for food, clothing, and shelter. They knew that large animals like buffalo thrived on grasslands, not in wooded forests. To stop trees from covering their hunting grounds, native peoples used an old weapon—fire.

These hunters had noticed how natural fires caused by lightning changed the land. Woodlands that had been destroyed by fire soon sprouted new growth of smaller plants. Buffalo, bear, deer, and turkey fed on new grasses, seeds, and berries that grew in burned areas. Juicy young plants were called "fire grass" in native languages.

Native tribes started their own fires to hold back forests and grow new fire grass. They also used fire as a hunting tool for herding large numbers of wild animals. Animals fleeing from man-made fires were rounded up and killed by experienced hunters. In this way, hundreds of miles of forest were destroyed each year.

Over thousands of years, fires changed North American lands. Repeated fires kept forests from growing across the middle of the continent. Long-grass prairies and short-grass plains were created and maintained by native tribes. Hunting tribes of the Plains pushed back the forest and expanded their hunting grounds in all directions. By the time Europeans arrived in the 1600s, the buffalo range reached east all the way to Pennsylvania.

Native Americans started fires to halt forest growth and create grazing land

Indian woodsmen cleared forest areas for villages and farmland

European settlers in the eastern forests found that some of the land had been cleared by Indian fires. Eastern tribes like the Pawhatans and Iroquois cleared land for both hunting and farming. Colonists in Jamestown, Virginia, found Indian villages of up to 200 people who farmed nearby fields. These were Indian woodsmen who lived in man-made clearings on the edge of the forest.

Fields of corn, beans, and squash were planted on cleared land near villages. Iroquois woodsmen built their homes, called longhouses, out of wood taken from nearby forests. They chopped down trees with stone axes and built the houses with pine logs and cedar bark.

Indian woodsmen cleared new sites for villages and fields every ten to twenty years. Newly cleared land had rich soil for growing crops. After years of planting, however, nutrients in the soil were used up by farm crops. Deserted fields were left behind and in time became enriched by new plant life. Old Indian fields were the first lands settled by pioneer woodsmen from Europe.

STONE AXES AND GIRDLED TREES

Indian woodsmen used stone axes to clear forests for villages and fields. In a process called "girdling," they carved deep rings around the bases of trees. These rings were like open wounds. Girdled trees soon died and lost their leaves, letting sunlight reach the ground below. Fields of corn were planted between the dead trees. In time, the dry, dead wood was easily chopped down and burned as firewood.

Girdling trees was one method of clearing forests

5

Pioneer Loggers

In the 1600s and 1700s, European settlers crossed the Atlantic Ocean to become the first pioneers in North America. They settled in colonies along the East Coast and moved inland from there. By 1720, there were 300,000 Europeans in the Eastern woodlands. As they cut trees and cleared land to make farms, these woodsmen became pioneer loggers.

Early settlers in New England and Pennsylvania found it easier to farm deserted Indian fields than to clear new land. Later settlers, however, had to clear woodlands for themselves to create farms.

In New England, these pioneer woodsmen bought land from the colonial government. But settlers in Pennsylvania, New York, and the southern forests didn't pay for their land. They moved to the edge of the frontier where there was no government control, picked an area they liked, and settled there. This was called squatting. Either way, pioneers had to clear land before farming it.

Pioneers cleared forests for farmland and used the logs to build homes

The most experienced woodsmen in colonial America had come from the forests of Germany and Sweden. They used straight-handled three-pound iron axes. By 1740, new American-style axes were produced in the colonies. The new axes had smaller, sharper cutting edges and a heavier axhead. Using these axes, woodsmen brought trees down quicker.

The pioneer woodsman chopped down, or "felled," trees by first notching an undercut with his ax on one side of the tree trunk. He then used strong, steady strokes to cut out chunks on the other side of the tree. He cut through toward his undercut until the tree toppled over. Wood snapped as the tree fell in the direction of the undercut. A strong axman could clear ten acres in a year, an area about the size of 7½ football fields.

ROYAL FORESTS AND TIMBER PIRATES

British forests were mostly used up by the time pioneer farmers were settling North America. England badly needed lumber and pine masts for navy ships. Starting in 1691, England's colonies in America were ordered to reserve certain pine forests for the royal navy. Pioneer loggers refused to obey these laws. They logged English timber for themselves and helped bring on the Revolutionary War.

Colonial "timber pirates" chopped down trees reserved for the English government

Pioneers labored to make room for planting fields. They called it "making land." The quickest way was to kill trees by girdling, then plant between the leafless trees. Girdling let in light, but left dead wood standing. The pioneer farmer used this method to get his first crops into the ground sooner. Later, he pulled out the stumps with an ox team. Land cleared with the ax and ox could be plowed and planted in long rows.

There were other reasons for making land by taking down trees. Fresh logs were used in home building, furniture making, and lumbering. Colonial sawmills paid farmers for logs to be cut into lumber. As the pioneer farmer began selling his extra logs, he became the pioneer logger of the eastern forests.

Pioneer loggers had a cash crop they hadn't even planted. They took down trees to supply shipbuilders, sawmills, and makers of wood products. Before the American Revolution, pioneer loggers supplied the British with lumber and wooden masts for sailing ships. They also collected tree sap and resins to produce tar, pitch, and turpentine for the British navy.

Northeastern farmers logged trees, tied them into rafts, and floated them down rivers for sale to the first water-powered sawmills in New England. It was the beginning of a new industry and the birth of a new North American laborer—the logger.

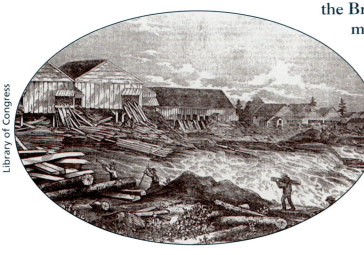

Farmers rafted logs down rivers to sawmills, where they were cut into lumber

7

Logging the Northeast

Logging farmers pioneered the lumber industry in the forests of the Northeast. During the 1700s, logging, lumber making, and shipbuilding became more important to the New England economy than farming. By 1800, pioneer woodsmen had turned from farming to logging and were called loggers and lumberjacks.

Loggers squatted land, felled trees, and sold logs. After the American Revolution, they bought 40-acre squares of forested U.S. government land. They set up logging camps in New England's deep woods and cut down white pine for miles around. Most of the cutting wasn't legal since the surrounding forest still belonged to the government, but many loggers ignored land laws.

Between 1810 and 1830, the U.S. population almost doubled. As cities used up local timber, deep woods loggers became their suppliers. Businessmen began buying up private woodlands in Maine, New Hampshire, and New York. They also stole timber from federal and state lands.

During the first half of the 1800s, businessmen formed logging companies and made logging into an industry. Logging company owners called lumbermen hired independent loggers to work for them. By the 1840s, New England's loggers were professional lumberjacks who worked for a monthly wage.

A Pennsylvania logging crew with their tools—axes, saws, and cant hooks

Forest Service Collection, National Agricultural Library

SOFTWOOD AND HARDWOOD FORESTS

Pine was the timber of choice in North American forests. In the Northeast, loggers cut all the white pine without bothering much about other trees. Softwoods like pine were valued in furniture making and lumbering. Straight-grained pines made sturdy masts for ships and boards that didn't warp. Lumberjacks in Maine cut only white pine until they ran out. Later, they went back and cut spruce, then turned to hardwoods like oak and maple.

New England lumberjacks worked all winter in the snow

Lumberjacks lived and worked in company logging camps through the cutting season. They cut in winter when it was easier to skid the logs out of the forest on the snow and ice. They spent five months in the deep woods working 12-hour days.

Loggers called "fallers" chopped down trees with axes, while "swampers" built forest roads. Logs were hauled by horse teams to the main roads on simple sleds called "go-devils" made of birch branches.

At the main roads, "cant-hook men" loaded logs onto large sleds using tools called cant hooks. Loads were piled high, balanced, and chained to the sleds, then pulled by oxen. Drivers called teamsters drove ox teams over the snow-packed roads.

On hills, roads were kept clear of snow or covered with hay and dirt to help brake the sled. On steep downhills, thick chains were tied around sled runners to slow the load. Logging roads led to the banks of frozen rivers and streams where sleds were unloaded. Men called "scalers" measured the logs and cut a company brand into the end of each one to mark ownership. Cant hook men then piled them along the banks for the log drive.

Some loggers stayed on for the drive while others returned to their farms. Those who stayed were the first year-round, full-time lumberjacks. They waited for spring thaw, when rivers ran deep with melted snow. This was the time for transporting, or "driving," logs to sawmills downriver.

Log drives were big business compared to the old rafting methods of pioneer loggers. Logging companies formed associations to build dams and to dig channels called sluices. Dams, gates, and sluices held water back or directed it certain ways to keep logs on the move. Rivers became public logging highways shared by different companies. And lumberjacks on the drive became "rivermen."

Smithsonian Institution

Lumberjacks hauled logs on sleds called go-devils

9

The Log Drive

Log drives on rushing rivers were the lumberjack's greatest adventure. Log drivers herded thousands of logs down rivers to sawmills, much as cowboys herded cattle along trails. Drivers rode standing on top of rushing logs to guide and transport them downriver. Only their spiked boots and quick feet kept them from toppling off of the wet, whirling logs.

Drivers were a special breed of lumberjack. They called themselves "rivermen" and "riverhogs." River drivers were dare-devil loggers. They worked hard, fought hard, and drank hard liquor when the drive was over.

A master driver planned the drive ahead of time, hired rivermen, and bossed the entire job. He had to know every bend, rock, and sandbar on the river. He was responsible for moving the logs downriver without them getting jammed into piles or swamped in shallow water to be left "high and dry."

In early spring, drive crews gathered on river banks with long-handled hooks called peaveys. They pulled logs loose from the frozen piles along the banks and rolled them into the rushing river. Log piles that were frozen solid were blasted apart with gunpowder by loggers called powder monkeys.

The thinnest and lightest logs were swept by currents to lead the way downriver. They were followed by a thickening stream of heavier logs that filled the waters behind. River crews included workers called drivers, jammers, and sackers. Drivers were the "cattiest," or most sure-footed, rivermen. They balanced on and held firm to pitching, rolling logs in spiked boots like cats with claws.

Jammers were sent ahead by the master driver to trouble spots downriver. They worked along the banks at tight bends and shallows to keep the logs moving and to prevent log jams. Sackers rode at the tail end of the drive, prying logs loose that had become stranded on rocks, islands, and bushes.

Log drivers using peaveys to push logs into the Swift Diamond River in New Hampshire

Library of Congress

Men and boys sorting logs at a riverside sawmill

On long drives, rivers flowed with millions of logs almost non-stop from April to June. Rivermen rode one drive after another down to sawmill towns and returned upstream by land. Long drives lasted days and sometimes weeks. Rivermen camped along the river banks and were supplied along the way by lumber company wagons called "wangans."

Everything from peavey hooks and camping gear to chewing tobacco and food was supplied by the wangan caravan, which included a cook wagon. Wangans often followed the drive on floating rafts.

Rivermen drove the churning, thundering herd of logs down to the sawmill into floating log fences called "booms." The booms trapped the logs and held them for sorting, like cattle in pens. Rivermen called sorters worked like river cowboys to separate logs by company brands. But instead of lasso ropes, they used long spiked tools called pike poles. When the work was done, rivermen "blew in" to town, spent their money, then headed back upstream to the next drive.

DEADLY LOG JAMS

Jams were huge pile-ups of logs that blocked drives downriver. Rivermen dreaded log jams the way cowboys feared cattle stampedes. A jam began as a few logs caught on rocks or shallows. Other logs soon piled up behind. To break the jam, rivermen climbed onto the tangle of logs, prying and poking with their peavey hooks at key logs. If this didn't loosen the jam, they blew it apart with dynamite. Many rivermen were crushed and killed in the sudden log stampede of a broken jam.

Rivermen sometimes used dynamite to break up a log jam

To the Great Lakes

The supply of white pine in New England was almost gone by 1840. Loggers moved on to New York and then Pennsylvania. But by 1860, there was little pine left to cut anywhere in the Northeast—and a new logging frontier was waiting to the west.

As early as 1836, lumbermen from Maine had begun buying up pine forests in Michigan, Minnesota, and Wisconsin. They hired men called "timber cruisers" to scout the forests and select the best pine woodlands. Over the next fifty years, logging in the states around the Great Lakes became big business.

Lumberjacks shouldered their axes and traveled west to the Great Lakes. On this new frontier they would learn new ways of logging. Logging methods changed during the 1860s as the United States entered the "machine age." New inventions, such as steam-powered engines, made the work of logging quicker and more efficient.

Logs filled the St. Croix River in Minnesota in 1905

The U.S. was a growing country with greater need for wood. Great Lakes lumberjacks cut trees to supply farmers with lumber for building homes and fences. Settlers on the treeless Great Plains also needed wood to burn for heating and cooking. Meanwhile, Great Lakes pine was in great demand in growing cities back East. The new railroads also needed wood to build tracks and bridges and as fuel for steam locomotives.

Lumbermen such as Frederick Weyerhaeuser hired lumberjacks to cut, haul, and transport Great Lakes pine. Loggers continued to cut trees by hand with axes. But in other ways, logging methods changed.

Logging in the Great Lakes states became big business in the 1800s

The simple go-devil sleds used back in Maine were replaced by "bummer carts." Lumberjacks chained one end of a log under the cart wheels to skid logs out to the main logging roads. At the main roads, logs were loaded onto large sleighs, which were bigger than the sleds used back East. Logging roads were also cut wider and covered with ice to make the heavy loads easier to pull.

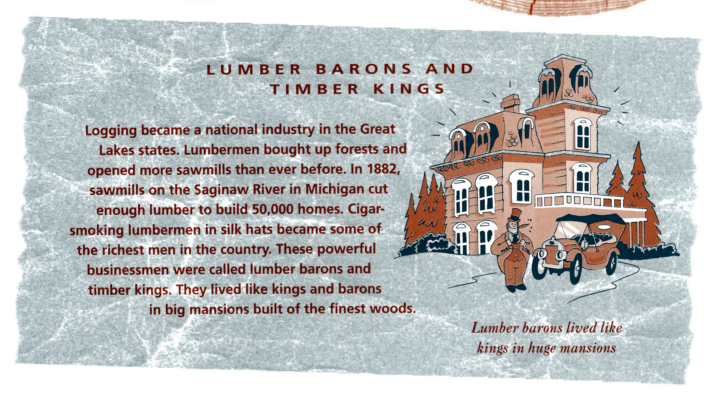

LUMBER BARONS AND TIMBER KINGS

Logging became a national industry in the Great Lakes states. Lumbermen bought up forests and opened more sawmills than ever before. In 1882, sawmills on the Saginaw River in Michigan cut enough lumber to build 50,000 homes. Cigar-smoking lumbermen in silk hats became some of the richest men in the country. These powerful businessmen were called lumber barons and timber kings. They lived like kings and barons in big mansions built of the finest woods.

Lumber barons lived like kings in huge mansions

At the end of the day, loggers called "road monkeys" sprinkled the roads with water. The water froze overnight, making the roads as smooth as glass. In the morning, they cut long grooves into the ice to guide sleigh runners. In the later years of Great Lakes logging, steam-powered tractors began to replace horse-pulled sleighs.

Logging railroads, another machine-age invention, were first used in Michigan during the 1870s. Steam locomotives hauled long trains loaded with logs over iron tracks. By 1887, 126 logging railroads carried pine out of Michigan forests. Logs were then unloaded and driven down rivers to distant sawmills.

During the 1890s, lumberjacks logged the last of the Great Lakes pine forests. The big lumber companies and steam-powered sawmills ran out of work—and wood. Loggers began moving south and farther west to other logging frontiers.

Railroad builders needed thousands of logs for railroad ties

River Rafting

Rafting was the main way of moving logs and lumber to market from the Great Lakes states. From the 1850s to the 1880s, giant rafts loaded with logs floated on rivers, lakes, and canals to lumber cities such as Albany, New York, and Chicago, Illinois. Loggers became raftsmen and river pilots. But rafting wasn't invented in the Lake States. It had started years earlier in the Northeast.

The first raftsmen were logging farmers. Beginning in the 1750s, they cleared land, cut logs, and then tied the logs into simple rafts. Rafts rode river currents downstream to mills and lumber yards. Sometimes entire families went along for the ride. They lived in huts on top of the rafts.

Rafting in the Great Lakes states was much different. Rafts were a lot bigger and were owned by lumbermen, not farmers. Lumber companies hired rafting crews to steer down the Mississippi River, the Erie Canal, and across the Great Lakes. Rafts grew to be three, four, and five acres in size—as big as three football fields.

Giant rafts moved more logs than the old-style log drives because rafts could be floated along canals and across lakes. Log drives were only useful on rushing rivers. Rafts could also carry loads of lumber and shingles for transport to market. So in the Lake states, rafts were favored over drives.

Loggers who built rafts first formed a frame made up of logs tied together. Other logs were packed inside the rectangular frame. The entire raft was held together by boards and ropes.

Rafting crews of up to 35 loggers steered the largest rafts. They used 50-foot-long oars to guide the raft on rivers, canals, and lakes. Oarsmen at the front of the raft were called fore oarsmen. Those at the back were aft oarsmen. A raft captain or pilot bossed the crew.

The raft pilot was like the master driver on log drives. He was responsible for getting logs to market without wrecking or getting stranded along the way. He watched for sandbars or shallow areas and tried to avoid them. If the raft became stranded on river bottoms, the crew waded into shallow water or fast-moving rapids to pry the raft free.

It took more than 6,000 logs to build this huge raft

Raftsmen played cards and sang songs on the trip down river

Raftsmen slept in small wooden huts built onto the rafts. They ate their meals on board in a cook shack. In calm, easy-flowing waters, raftsmen could relax. They played cards and checkers, made music, and swapped stories. At port towns along the way, raftsmen went ashore to visit bars and stay at hotels.

By the 1870s, rafting was modernized. Oarsmen were replaced by steam-powered tow boats and pushers. Rafts were towed or pushed by steamboats along lakes, rivers, and canals. Rafting crews required fewer men as rafts were steered by boats tied to guide ropes.

After delivering the rafts to mills and lumber towns, raftsmen were paid their wages. They spent their hard-earned money in bars and gambling houses, then headed back upstream.

CONTINENTAL LOG TRANSPORT SYSTEM

Great Lakes pine forests supplied lumber to far-away towns and cities. Logs were moved by raft in all directions along waterways. The Erie Canal carried rafts 325 miles east from Lake Erie to the big lumber town of Albany, New York. Chicago was another lumber center. Rafts traveled along rivers in Wisconsin and Michigan, then crossed Lake Michigan to Chicago. Rafts also went south down the Mississippi River all the way to lumber markets in New Orleans.

Loggers putting rafts together on the Susquehanna River

The Lumberjack

Lumberjacks chopped, hauled, and sawed wood 12 hours a day. They were always on the move from one forest to the next. The lumberjack felled trees, skidded them from the deep forest, and moved them by waterways and railroads.

Pioneer loggers in the U.S. came from England, Ireland, Scotland, Germany, and France. They brought axes, handsaws, and other simple woodworking tools. They also came with the dream of owning their own farms.

Pioneer loggers supplied the American colonies with wood for building and heating. They also supplied England and other countries. The English especially needed wood from North America. But there weren't enough loggers in the colonies to cut all the wood England wanted.

So the English government hired loggers from other countries to go to North America. In 1708, England sent shiploads of German immigrants to New York. The German loggers cut trees for England and used the cleared land for their own farms.

By the 1790s, businessmen in Northeastern cities were buying forest lands in Maine. They brought experienced loggers from Ireland and Scotland to cut pine in Maine's forests. They also hired French-Canadian loggers.

Choppers used handaxes to chop down trees

BANGOR TIGERS AND TIMBER BEASTS

River drivers from Maine called themselves Bangor Tigers after the big logging town of Bangor, Maine. Like tigers or cats with claws, Bangor Tigers rode logs in spiked boots. They were daredevils known for tough work and hard drinking. In time, all lumberjacks from East to West were known and sometimes feared as "roughnecks," "timber beasts," and "wildcats." They labored hard, fought hard, and went on drunken sprees in lumber towns.

A logger sitting on a felled tree, around 1915

16

Lumberjacks taking a lunch break

The sons of these pioneer loggers were the first American-born, or "Yankee," lumberjacks. They left family farms to work in winter logging camps. There they cut down forests owned by the first U.S. logging companies.

Loggers who cut down trees with hand-axes were called "choppers." The job they did was known as "falling" or "felling" trees. Other loggers called "buckers" trimmed off branches and cut trees into logs. In the spring, rivermen drove logs downriver to sawmills.

While Yankee loggers worked the forests and rivers of New England, German lumberjacks logged Pennsylvania pine. These so-called Pennsylvania "Dutch" loggers were joined by Irish, French-Canadian, and Yankee loggers as the logging frontier shifted west.

Lumbermen in the Lake states also brought more loggers from Europe. Experienced loggers from the forests of Sweden, Norway, and Finland cut Great Lakes pine. They also worked the big company sawmills, cutting logs into lumber.

Lumberjacks were kept on the move, following the pine. For this reason, they were mostly single men without families of their own. Their only homes were logging camps in the deep woods. Loggers owned no land and had few possessions, except for their bedrolls. Since bedrolls were also called bindles, loggers became known as "bindle stiffs." Stiff was a word meaning wandering laborer.

In the South, lumbermen hired Mexicans and African Americans to work the hardest jobs in the bald cypress swamps. In the West, Japanese, Greeks, and Italians joined other loggers cutting redwood and fir trees. They worked as fallers, peelers, and buckers. They felled trees, peeled off bark, and cut or "bucked" giant redwoods into short logs. They also worked as bull whackers driving ox teams and as sawyers, operating machines in steam-powered sawmills.

Loggers in the South worked in baldcypress swamps where dangerous snakes and crocodiles lived

The Logger's Gear

The logger's gear included his basic tools and work clothes. Though he owned his clothes and boots, the lumberjack owned little else. His ax, saw, and other tools were owned by the logging company that paid him. But the logger cleaned and sharpened his cutting tools as if they were his own.

The first pioneer loggers had come to North America with their own tools. German and Irish loggers chopped down Northeastern pine with long, straight-handled axes. The front of the axhead, called the bit, flared out to a wide cutting edge. The back of the axhead, called the poll, was narrow and thin. This ax looked like an ancient European war ax, weighed only three pounds, and made shallow cuts.

Colonial axmakers in New England, Pennsylvania, and North Carolina improved the European ax. They made heavy, seven-pound iron axheads with sharp steel cutting edges. The new American axes had thinner handles and thicker, heavier polls. In the cold Northeast where loggers wore gloves, ax handles were thin for a tighter grip. Loggers in the warm South used thicker ax handles.

Loggers in the West were the first to use saws for felling trees. In the East, saws were seldom used for cutting down trees. Axes cut through soft eastern pine quickly enough. But western loggers found it quicker to cut down giant redwoods with 18-foot falling saws. The saw blades were narrow and thin to slice through wood more easily.

To keep blades from jamming in the sawcuts, loggers drove steel wedges into sawcuts with wooden sledge hammers. The wedges kept sawcuts open and helped the saw blades move freely. To keep saws from sticking in pine sap, loggers squirted kerosene into the cuts to thin the sap. They carried the liquid in rum bottles or oil cans, which they hung from branches while they worked.

Axes, saws, wedges, and sledges were the basic tools of loggers who felled trees and cut them into logs. Loggers used other tools to load logs onto sleds and carts and to drive them down rivers. These tools were called cant hooks and peaveys.

A loggers' spiked boots, canvas pants, and razor sharp tools helped him do his job well

Loggers used a truck with sled runners to haul logs through the snow

Cant hooks were five-foot long wooden poles with iron hooks on the end. Loggers used them to roll logs on the ground and load them onto sleds or carts. Peaveys were longer poles with both a hook and spike on the end. Rivermen depended on peaveys on the log drive downriver. They were the basic tool of the riverman on the log drive. The pointed spike was needed to poke and move free-floating logs. The hook was used to grab logs and pull them out of the water or push them in.

All loggers, no matter what job they did, needed spiked boots. Lumberjacks called them calked boots. Calk is another word for a pointed metal spike. Spiked boots dug into wood to give loggers footing while they worked. Rivermen used them to walk and balance on rushing logs. Spiked boots gripped like tiger claws and gave lumberjacks the name "timber tigers."

Machines made the work of logging easier and quicker

Horse-drawn carts began to be replaced by trucks and other machines

THE LOGGER'S CLOTHES

A logger kept all of what he owned in a canvas sack. Into the sack went clothes, gloves, and personal items. Loggers wore long woolen underwear, heavy socks, and wool pants held up by canvas suspenders. They rolled or trimmed their pant legs up to keep them clear of tools and machinery. Western loggers wore water-proof canvas pants called tin pants. Loggers also wore heavy shirts called mackinaws, sometimes two at a time for warmth.

The Logging Camp

Loggers worked and lived in camps owned by logging companies. Logging camps were located in the deep woods close to timberlands. As timberlands were cleared of pine, camps were abandoned. Loggers moved from one temporary camp to the next. Home was a bunkhouse in a forest clearing.

The first logging camps in New England housed thirty to fifty men. The camp was little more than a bunkhouse built of logs, which loggers called a shanty. Early loggers liked to call themselves "shantyboys" after these bunkhouse shacks.

Outside the cookhouse at a Minnesota logging camp

Long rows of bunk beds lined opposite walls of a shanty. Loggers padded their bunks with hay and slept in their own blankets, called bedrolls. Some drilled small holes in the wall near their bunks for fresh air.

In front of each row of bunks were long benches made from split logs, called deacon seats. At the center of the shanty was a fire pit made of sand and stone. Smoke escaped through a hole in the roof.

The earliest shanties served as both bunkhouse and cookhouse. Camp cooks made meals over the fire pit, cooking up stews in large kettles. Soon, though, logging camps had separate cookhouses with dining rooms. Dining room tables were made of pine boards, cut by the loggers themselves.

By the mid-1800s, open fire pits were replaced by cast-iron wood stoves. Stovepipes carried smoke directly outside, making it easier for loggers to breathe inside. But bunkhouse air was still damp and smelly from dirty clothes and hanging laundry. Loggers washed their underwear and socks, then hung them to dry on the stove.

Dirty clothes and drying laundry made bunkhouse air stuffy and smelly

LOGGER REST AND RELAXATION

Loggers worked 12 hours a day, six days a week. They had a 9 o'clock curfew that meant lights out and to bed. On Saturday night, however, there was no curfew. Loggers stayed awake playing cards, telling stories and singing songs, or playing instruments. Some danced jigs and reels. Sunday was a day of rest. Loggers read a picture magazine called the Police Gazette, sharpened tools, mended and washed clothes,

Bunkhouses at a winter logging camp in Minnesota

The logging camp blacksmith sharpened and repaired tools

The bunkhouse also had a foot-powered grindstone that loggers used to sharpen their cutting tools. Water dripped from a trough to cool the stone as it got hot from the friction of sharpening. By morning, puddles from the dripping grindstone turned to ice.

Loggers were awakened before daylight by the camp cook. He beat an iron triangle, blew a horn, or shouted curses to wake the men and call them to breakfast. Loggers washed with strong soap and cold water from a barrel. Then they went over to the cookhouse.

Breakfast was pancakes, eggs, beans, potatoes, and fried pork or bacon. Lumberjacks washed it all down with black coffee and prune pie. Then they lit their pipes and waited for daylight. Meanwhile, teamsters hitched their ox or horse teams to sleds or wagons. At first light, loggers shouldered their tools and headed for the timberlands.

Loggers had their own name for the timberlands where they cut trees. They called it the "choppings." Lumberjacks labored until noon and the midday meal. The cook brought lunch out to the choppings by one-horse bobsled. He handed out tin plates and dished out the food—cold biscuits, pork, and stew.

In the South and West, logging camps grew in size. One camp could have several shanties. By the 1880s, logging companies settled entire towns with loggers and sometimes loggers' families.

21

Logging Down South

Lumber companies sent timber cruisers south to scout pine forests during the 1880s. There they found more pine than ever before. Texas alone had almost as many pine trees as the three Lake states combined. Loggers shouldered their axes once again, and this time they headed south.

Logging in the South had actually started years earlier. In colonial times, southern farmers logged and rafted pine as pioneer woodsmen had done in the Northeast. In the mid-1800s, logging in the South grew into a regional industry. But it wasn't until the 1890s that southern logging became a national industry, supplying other parts of the country with timber.

During the 1880s, Great Lakes lumber barons began buying huge forests of southern pine. By 1885, almost 32 million acres of forest had been sold in Texas—an area about the size of New York state. Rich lumbermen from the North would soon become even richer in the South.

Lumberjacks in the South had to learn new methods of logging. The warm southern climate was much different than the icy cold Northeast and Lake states. Sleds and sleighs could no longer be used. There were other differences too.

The Mississippi River flowed south. However, the big lumber markets were in the North. It didn't pay to raft logs against the current. Some logs were rafted or driven on rivers east to the Atlantic Ocean. Steamboats then carried them north up the coast. But lumbermen soon found a better way to transport their timber.

West Virginia loggers with their tools, around 1890

COMPANY TOWNS

Loggers and logging camps went through many changes in the South. The winter logging camp of the northern forests became the company town in the South. Lumber companies in the southern states owned forests, mills, and entire towns. Lumberjacks lived in company towns and cut company timber all year round. They were paid in coupons instead of money and they had to shop at company stores. Loggers were forced to pay two weeks' wages for a pair of boots.

Loggers often paid two weeks' wages for a pair of boots at the company store

22

Pull boats moved logs along waterways in the South

During the 1890s, railroads were built through the South connecting southern forests to lumber markets up North. These main-line railroads covered hundreds of miles. Smaller logging railroads were also built to carry logs from the forests to the main lines.

There were other changes too. Parts of the South weren't just hotter than the North, they were wetter as well. In flooded swamp lands, loggers learned to cut and haul bald cypress trees. Like pine, bald cypress lumber was strong and didn't warp easily.

After 1890, loggers called swampers used a new invention called the pull-boat. Pull-boats were simple flat-bottomed boats with steam-powered engines mounted on top. The engines pulled steel cables that were tied to felled trees. Logs were pulled from the swamps, gathered in log ponds, then moved to market along waterways.

In the pine forests, lumberjacks continued to use bummer carts to haul logs on land. Some of these carts had big 12-foot wheels and were called caralogs. Logs were skidded out to clearings and then loaded onto railroad cars for transport to market.

A method called power skidding was also used in the southern pine forests. Power skidding on land was similar to pull-boat logging in the swamps. Loggers tied steel cables to felled pines and used steam-engines to haul the logs in toward the skidder. Over time, power skidders replaced carts and caralogs.

Logging in the South continued into the 1920s and later. However, fewer and fewer pine trees were left. Meanwhile, another logging frontier was opening up, far to the west near the Pacific Ocean.

Carts with giant wheels were used to move huge tree trunks

23

Logging Out West

While some loggers went south during the 1890s, others headed west. Giant forests in California, Oregon, and Washington state soon fell under the logger's ax. By 1900, the western forests had become the last great logging frontier in the U.S.

Indians on the Northwest coast were the first to log tall western trees. They carved huge canoes and totem poles from the giant logs. In the 1830s, businessmen from England set up the first sawmill in the Northwest. They sawed Douglas fir logs and shipped the lumber over the Pacific Ocean to foreign countries.

After gold was discovered in California in 1848, gold seekers rushed in from around the world. Lumber was needed to build mining towns and homes.

During the 1850s, logging companies set up mills along the coasts of Washington, Oregon, and California. Water-powered mills sawed giant redwoods and Douglas fir. Loggers hauled logs to the mills on ox-carts. From the mills, lumber was sent down long wooden chutes and loaded onto boats. San Francisco soon became the biggest lumber and shipping center in the West.

Northwest Indians carved canoes and tall totem poles from giant logs

From the 1860s to the 1890s, West Coast loggers supplied lumber mostly to California towns and foreign countries. Logging out West didn't become a national industry until cross-country railroads reached into the western forests. Only then could lumber be transported cheaply across the country.

During the 1890s, timber cruisers rode railroads into the western forests. In 1900, lumberman Frederick Weyerhaeuser bought 900,000 acres of Douglas fir from the Northern Pacific Railroad. Lumberjacks were soon cutting the last logging frontier to supply the nation with lumber.

Western lumberjacks hauled logs from the forest on logging railroads

West Coast redwood, sequoia, and fir trees stood 250 feet tall—150 feet taller than eastern pines. Loggers had to cut through trees that were 13 feet thick. Since trees spread wider at the ground, loggers found it easier to chop 10 or 12 feet up the trunk. They cut notches into the tree and inserted platforms called springboards. Loggers stood on these springboards as they cut.

Some redwoods were so huge that a wagon could drive through a tunnel carved in its trunk

Special long-handled axes cut deeper into thick trees. In the West, loggers also began felling trees with crosscut saws. They found that starting cuts with axes and finishing them with saws was the quickest way to cut through the giant trees.

Machine age inventions were used in the West at the same time they were used in the South. Western loggers used steam engines for power skidding as southern loggers did. On steep mountain slopes, they also used a method called high-lead logging. Logs were hauled through the air on steel cables using steam power, tree poles, and pulley wheels. They were then loaded onto logging railroads for transport to mills.

After 1920, the West supplied the U.S. with more lumber than any other logging region. Since the 1950s, almost half of all U.S. lumber comes from the West.

SKIDROADS, CHUTES, AND FLUMES

Logging in the warmer mountains of the West required new methods. Early western loggers built roads out of logs. These roads, called skidroads, were then greased to help ox teams skid logs out of the forest. Later inventions like chutes and flumes did a better job. Chutes were long troughs carved out of logs and laid end to end. They carried logs down steep mountainsides by the force of gravity. Flumes were like chutes, but also used water to speed logs along.

Flumes filled with water carried logs down mountainsides

25

Logging Railroads

Railroads brought big changes to the logging frontiers. From the 1870s to the 1890s, railroads began reaching into forests of the Lake states, the South, and the West. Steam-powered locomotives hauled huge loads of logs to mills and lumber to markets. Log drives and rafting became transport methods of the past.

The nation's first railroads were built in the eastern states during the 1830s through the 1850s. Trains carried passengers and hauled freight between cities. The first cross-country railroad was completed in 1869. But railroads weren't used for logging until the 1870s.

The nation's first logging railroads carried logs from the forests of Michigan. These railroads ran on temporary tracks and hauled logs short distances from the deep forest. Permanent main-line railroads then carried the logs over longer distances to mills and lumber markets. After an area of forest was cut and cleared, loggers moved the railroad tracks to a new area.

This logging train carried logs from Georgia's forests to sawmills

Rafting was still the main method of moving logs and lumber in the Lake states through the 1890s. By 1900, though, more lumber reached Chicago markets by railroad than by raft. When loggers and lumbermen moved south to log southern pine, railroads became even more important.

The South didn't have a network of lakes, rivers, and canals for rafting or driving logs. Railroads were needed for moving logs and lumber to markets up north. Between 1865 and 1910, almost 30,000 miles of main-line track were laid through the South.

Meanwhile, loggers laid thousands of miles of temporary logging railroads in the deep woods. By 1910, there were 1,400 miles of logging track in Texas alone. Main-line railroads built special spur lines into the forests to reach distant logging lines.

RAILROADS AND WOOD

From the start, railroads depended on wood to keep running. Locomotive engines were powered by steam that was produced by burning wood to heat water in the engine's boiler. Railroads also needed wood for building tracks and train cars. Tracks were laid on wooden crossties cut from hardwoods like oak and walnut. In 1869, railroads used more than 2 million acres of trees—an area 2½ times the size of Rhode Island.

Locomotive steam engines burned wood to heat water in the engine's boiler

Cross-country railroads first reached the western forests in the 1880s and 1890s. In 1883, the Northern Pacific Railroad connected Minnesota to Oregon with 1,700 miles of track. Cross-country railroads offered a way to move western lumber to eastern markets. Only then did Great Lakes lumbermen move west. They bought western forest lands owned by the railroads.

Railroads and other machine-age inventions speeded up logging in the South and West. An invention called the self-loader was first used in Alabama. The self-loader was a steam-powered crane that ran on tracks atop railroad flatcars. Logs were tied to cables, then hauled up by the crane and loaded onto flatcars. As each flatcar was filled with logs, the self-loader moved on its tracks to the next empty car.

In 1908, loggers began using another invention called the portable skidding tower. The skidding tower was a crane mounted on a flatcar. The crane hauled logs tied to cables and self-loaded them onto train cars.

Networks of main-lines, spurs, and logging railroads carried logs from forests to mills. Steam-powered mills were located along main-line tracks. Logs were cut into lumber, then loaded back onto main-line railroads for transport to distant markets.

Loggers using a self-loader to stack logs on a railroad flatcar

At the Sawmill

Sawmills were like frontier factories. Mill workers called sawyers cut logs into lumber, beams, shingles, and other wood products. Without sawmills to cut logs by machine, logging would never have become a national industry.

Early loggers sawed their own logs into boards by hand with long-bladed handsaws. But processing wood by hand took too much time and muscle.

In 1631, the first water-powered sawmill in the U.S. was built on the Salmon Falls River in Maine. Rushing water turned the sawmill's waterwheel. The wheel then turned a crank which moved a long saw up and down. In this way, water power was used to make mechanical power to run the saw. Water-powered sawmills cut 25 times more lumber than loggers could saw by hand.

Early mills were small family businesses built on local rivers. One or two sawyers pushed and guided logs through the mechanical saw by hand or used simple carriers. Carriers were long narrow tables. Logs were moved along a carrier by hand-turned cranks.

By 1840, there were more than 30,000 sawmills in the U.S. They were still mostly small, water-powered mills. But times were changing. New machine-age inventions like steam power would soon turn logging and lumbering into a national industry.

Mechanical saws quickly cut logs into boards of lumber

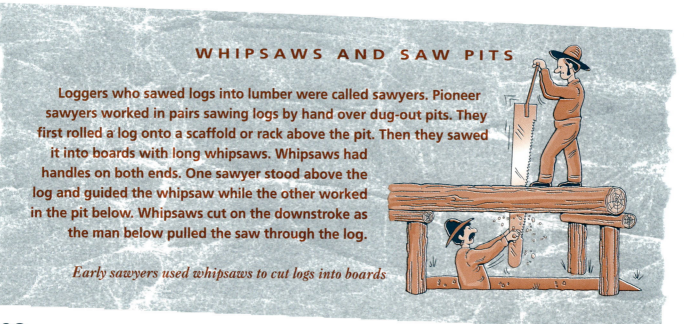

WHIPSAWS AND SAW PITS

Loggers who sawed logs into lumber were called sawyers. Pioneer sawyers worked in pairs sawing logs by hand over dug-out pits. They first rolled a log onto a scaffold or rack above the pit. Then they sawed it into boards with long whipsaws. Whipsaws had handles on both ends. One sawyer stood above the log and guided the whipsaw while the other worked in the pit below. Whipsaws cut on the downstroke as the man below pulled the saw through the log.

Early sawyers used whipsaws to cut logs into boards

Workers at a Minnesota sawmill, around 1890

Steam-powered mills used steam instead of water to make mechanical energy. The force of steam turned wheels and cranks. A New Orleans mill ran on steam as early as 1811. However, small water-powered mills outnumbered steam mills until the 1870s.

Logging became a national industry in the Lake states during the 1870s. Logging companies built big steam-powered sawmills to keep up with demand for lumber. One Michigan mill employed 350 sawyers who worked in shifts by day and night. In winter, steam was run through pipes into mill ponds to keep them from freezing.

New inventions helped the mills work faster. Automatic conveyor belts carried logs from ponds outside the sawmill directly to the saw. Saws changed too. Single up-and-down saws were replaced by gang saws with six to thirty blades. Gang saws cut logs into many boards all at once.

Circular saws began replacing up-and-down saws around the 1850s. By the 1870s, double circular saws were used to cut through big logs. One saw cut from above and the other from below. In the West, giant redwood logs were cut by four-bladed circular saws called breaking down saws.

In the 1880s, western sawyers began using band saws to cut redwood logs. A single band blade was wound around and turned by two wheels. Band saws cut with one long non-stop motion.

As railroads entered the woods and steam replaced water power, mills were located along railroads instead of rivers. In time, more and more automatic machinery was used to finish and smooth lumber.

A team of oxen hauls logs out of the Oregon forest on a skid road

The Dangers of Logging

Logging was the most dangerous work on the frontier. Almost 200 loggers died from work accidents each year. Many more were injured. Loggers were crushed by trees, drowned on drives, and flattened under log piles in train and sled accidents. Every job, from chopping down trees to working in sawmills, was dangerous.

Tree choppers, called fallers, faced the dangers first. After chopping or sawing through a tree, fallers shouted, "Timber!" This warned other loggers to watch out for falling trees. Fallers also jumped out of the way, since cut trees didn't always fall straight.

Many loggers were injured or killed by kickbacks

Cut trees sometimes tangled and caught in other trees on the way down. When this happened, the cut base of the tree skipped backward on the stump. Loggers called this a "kickback." Fallers who didn't jump to safety quickly enough were smashed and killed. A faller named Johnson was killed by a kickback in 1896. He was swept downhill by a falling tree and broke his back.

Hauling logs was dangerous work too. Ox or horse teams pulled sleds piled high with logs over icy roads. Even talented teamsters sometimes lost control of sleds on steep hills. A heavy sled could slide forward faster than the animals could pull it. Runaway sleds crushed animals and their drivers.

No logging job was more dangerous than log driving. Rivermen began the drive by pushing logs from riverbank landings into the rushing water. Even with heavy spiked boots on their feet, rivermen often slipped and fell into the rush of logs.

The ride downriver was more risky. Drivers rode, walked, and leaped from one log to another to keep them all moving. One wrong step could tumble a driver into a log stampede. Few loggers could swim, and their heavy boots and wool clothes dragged them down.

Many sawmill workers lost fingers and limbs to blades such as this giant cutoff saw

Log jams were the greatest danger. Loggers had to climb over the tangled mountain of logs to yank them free. As a jam came loose, logs broke free and rushed forward like an avalanche. Drivers scrambled for safety over the crashing logs. But they didn't always make it.

Riverman Pete Hurd died in a jam on the Connecticut River in 1901. After breaking the jam by freeing the key log, he was swept forward, thrown into the air, then crushed between logs.

When logging entered the machine age, accidents increased. New inventions like steam-driven saws, railroads, and power skidders brought new dangers. Steel cables sometimes snapped and lashed out, cutting and killing loggers. High climbers and riggers who set high-lead cables could be blown off treetops by wind or knocked off by flying pulleys, chains, and hooks. Logging trains, which had no brakes, sometimes jumped the tracks and rolled over loggers.

Sawmill machinery like gang saws, log carriages, and band saws often cut off loggers' fingers, hands, and arms. Mill workers also got lung diseases from breathing sawdust. Loggers weren't protected by safety laws until the 1900s. Between 1870 and 1910, at least 7,500 loggers died on the job.

"Tree topping" was a very dangerous job. When the top of the tree snapped off, the trunk vibrated violently, sometimes throwing the logger to his death.

FOREST FIRES

Loggers were helpless when fires started in the deep woods. Fire was a problem mostly in the hot, dry forests of the West. Stray sparks from steam engines, logging trains, and even loggers' pipes could start a blaze. During the dry season of 1902, fires raged through western woodlands from Canada to California. Almost a million acres of timber were burned in 110 separate fires. Loggers floated on logs and rafts in lakes and rivers to escape the flames.

The Lumber Towns

Lumber towns grew up around sawmills. Logs were transported to lumber towns for sawing into lumber. Some towns like Albany, New York, and Chicago, Illinois, became nation-wide centers of the logging industry. Smaller towns like Bangor, Maine, were regional centers. All were playgrounds for log drivers, raftsmen, and other loggers.

When loggers went to town, they said they were "blowin' in." They rode fast or, "blew in," off the river. They would also spend, or "blow," their money quickly. Bangor was one of the first lumber towns where loggers celebrated after many months of hard labor.

Bangor was located on Maine's Penobscot River. Bangor sawmills cut lumber, then shipped it to market by boat. Loggers crossed paths with sailors in saloons and dance halls on Bangor's Haymarket Square. After drinking and dancing with showgirls, loggers often ended their nights in fights with sailors.

New England lumberjacks also visited larger towns like Portland, Maine and Boston, Massachusetts. But most loggers favored towns closer to home. New Hampshire loggers on the Androscoggin River liked to blow in at Nat Leach's Umbagog House.

Lumber towns were built along rivers and waterways

The Umbagog House was a hotel with 42 rooms and a large saloon. During the log driving season, Nat Leach put up as many as 90 loggers a night. When the rooms filled up, lumberjacks slept in bedrolls on hallway floors.

Lumber towns in the Lake States were bigger and rowdier than New England towns. More than 75 sawmills worked day and night cutting lumber at Saginaw, Michigan. Rivermen drove and rafted logs down the Saginaw River.

Lumberjacks and sailors sometimes didn't get along very well

SKID ROAD TOWNS

Western loggers built logging roads out of cut logs called skid roads. The first skid road led to a sawmill in Seattle. As Seattle grew, the skid road became a street of saloons and dance halls. In time, Skid Road came to mean the rowdy streets of any lumber town. Humboldt's Saloon in the Skid Road town of Aberdeen, Washington, was a favorite logger hang-out. Its wood floors were so splintered by loggers' spiked boots that they had to be replaced twice a year.

As many as 5,000 loggers sometimes blew in at Saginaw on a single night. The first thing a logger did was get a haircut and a shave. Then he bought a new pair of boots and maybe a "Sunday suit" at Little Jake's Clothing Store, for dressing up while in town.

The saloons, theaters, and dance halls in Saginaw were on Genesee Street. When loggers had enough of the theater shows and too much to drink, they often started fighting. One sawmill worker named George Lavigne graduated from street fighting to professional boxing. From 1893 to 1899, Lavigne was the lightweight champion of the world and was called the Saginaw Kid.

Great Lakes lumber towns were big, but not as wild as towns in the West. Portland, Oregon, and Seattle, Washington, were lumber towns on the Pacific Ocean. They shipped lumber by sea and also by railroad. Loggers who blew in at these towns shared saloons and hotels with sailors, miners, and fishermen.

Erickson's saloon in Portland had the biggest bar in the West. It also had the biggest bouncer, the 300-pound Jumbo Reilly—and the biggest bulletin board. Loggers left notes and messages to long-lost pals on Erickson's cork board.

California's redwood loggers blew in at Eureka on Humboldt Bay. San Francisco had a rowdy section of town called the Barbary Coast, but loggers preferred Eureka. It was closer to the redwoods.

Chicago's lumber district was one of the centers of the logging industry

Tall Tales and Ballads

At night in bunkhouses, loggers swapped stories and songs. They sat on long benches called deacon seats and took turns telling tales or singing story songs called ballads. Loggers sang about their work, their heroes, and dangers of the deep woods. They told of strange creatures, contests of strength, ghosts, and giants.

Some tales were true or partly true stories of real loggers and their work. Others were made-up stories called tall tales. Loggers used tall tales to stretch the facts about logging and its dangers. The tallest tales of all were about a giant logger called Paul Bunyan.

It was said that Paul Bunyan stood taller than the giant redwoods. He cut down whole forests with his three-mile-long saw. While heading out West, he dragged his peavey pole behind him and dug out the Grand Canyon.

Some of the Paul Bunyan tales were told as jokes meant to tease young loggers. New loggers were called "greenhorns," after the green stubby horns of a young ox. No logger could ever hope to do the work of Paul Bunyan. But young greenhorns with blistered hands sat wide-eyed and listened. If they couldn't be Paul Bunyan, maybe they could be a real-life hero like Jim Stewart.

Loggers told tall tales about giant logger Paul Bunyan and his huge ox Babe

TALES OF FIGHTING MEN

Lake states loggers told stories of a fighting logger named John Driscoll. They called him Silver Jack for his white hair. While many loggers got into drunken fights in lumber towns, none could win against Silver Jack. They said he could twist horseshoes in his bare hands and punch out an ox with one fist. He beat Joe Fournier in a day-long saloon fight in Michigan. Witnesses said the Red Keg Saloon shook like an earthquake when the fighters butted heads.

Lumberjacks' tall tales matched the size of the trees they chopped down

34

Jim Stewart was champion at the sport of logrolling, which lumberjacks called birling. In birling, two lumberjacks stood on a floating log and turned it with their feet. The one who fell off first was the loser. Though Stewart was a real person and a talented birler, stories about him stretched the truth.

Loggers told of the time Jim Stewart faced off with Tom Oliver in a Lake states birling contest. Three thousand loggers watched them birl for two days—the longest contest ever. Stewart finally won when Oliver grew tired and collapsed.

Loggers also told tales of a strange forest creature called the Hodag. They said it had the face of a lion, the horns of an ox, and the spiny back and tail of a dinosaur. Greenhorn loggers hoped to never see one. But there were greater and more real dangers for them to worry about—like log jams.

The most popular logger ballad, called "The Jam on Gerry's Rocks," was sung about a log jam that killed seven young rivermen.

Birlers competed to see who could balance longer on a spinning log

It was on a Sunday morning as you shall quickly hear,
Our logs were piled up mountain high, we could not keep them clear,
"Turn out, brave boys," the foreman cried, without a voice of fear,
"We'll break the jam on Gerry's Rocks and for Saginaw we'll steer."

. . . They had not rolled off many logs before the boss did say,
"I would you all be on your guard, for the jam will soon give way,"
He had no more than spoke his words when the jam did break and go,
And carried off those six brave lads and the foreman, young Monroe.

Loggers risked their lives each day. Those who survived the dangers lived to tell the tales.

Young loggers feared the legendary Hodag forest creature

Famous Loggers

Though thousands of men logged America's forests, few became famous. Only the best loggers were talked about. On each frontier, loggers knew the names of the best axmen, master drivers, and camp foremen. They were the strongest, most skilled, and most daring men of the deep woods.

From 1864 to 1887, John Ross was a master driver on the Penobscot and Kennebec rivers in Maine. Ross was so famous as a riverman that a steamboat was named after him. Rivermen also sang a song about him.

In the song, Ross is remembered as a hard-driving river boss who worked his crews like slaves. He pulled one riverman out of bed on his wedding day to work a long drive. Nothing mattered more to Ross than driving logs downriver.

Perley Hurd was another famous master driver. He bossed long drives down the Connecticut River through New Hampshire and Vermont.

Hurd was one of the "cattiest" rivermen in New England. He had the balance and nine lives of a cat. He could jump straight up from a fast-moving log and land on a center jam. Center jams were piles of moving logs tangled at the center of a river. Hurd could untangle center jams by himself.

An axman named Logger Bradbury was famous in the Columbia River country of Oregon. Bradbury arrived in Oregon in 1847 after traveling west from the forests of Maine.

Nearly twenty loggers could fit on the stump of this giant tree

Logger Bradbury learned the hard way not to chop too close to the base of a fir tree

36

When Bradbury chopped at the base of his first giant fir, sap ran out and stuck to his ax. It was more sap than he'd ever seen. Bradbury had to stop cutting and wait for the sap to stop flowing. In time, he learned to cut high above the base of western fir trees to avoid the sap that collected there.

No one was more famous in Maine's woods than Jigger Jones. Jones was an expert axman and camp foreman for over 40 years. He was a small man, but powerful and quick on his feet. He wore long underwear, heavy pants, and nothing else. He worked barefooted in deep snow, but never seemed to feel the cold.

Jones was born in the 1870s and went to work as a camp cook's helper at the age of 12. Within a few years, he graduated to chopping down trees and driving ox teams. By the time he was 20, Jones was made foreman of a camp on the Androscoggin River. Because he was so small, he had to fight and win against much bigger men to gain their respect.

Small scars called "loggers' smallpox" covered Jones's body from his chest down. They were made by the spiked boots of loggers who had jumped on Jones in fights. Jones took a beating, but never lost. He also survived many accidents. He survived a 45-foot fall off a dam and a sled wreck that killed three horses. There was no better foreman, or "bull of the woods," than Jigger Jones.

Jigger Jones never wore shoes— even in deep snow

FAMOUS CAMP COOKS

Camp cooks were almost as important as camp foremen. Good food fueled the work of loggers and kept them happy. A bad cook could cause loggers to quit a camp and move on. Tom Bracket was a famous camp cook in New England. He made mouth-watering stews, puddings, doughnuts, and pies. Joe Boulay was also famous, but not for his cooking. Loggers called him Dirty Joe because he seldom washed himself or his clothes. His food tasted okay, as long as loggers looked at their food and not at Dirty Joe.

The Lumber Barons

Logging became a nationwide industry in the Lake States. The small, family-owned logging companies of the Northeast became big businesses in the Great Lakes forests. Lumbermen like Frederick Weyerhaeuser and Isaac Stephenson became millionaires. They owned whole forests, rafting companies, and sawmills. Because they were so wealthy, people called them "lumber barons" and "timber kings."

Isaac Stephenson was born in 1829 into a Canadian logging family. By the time he was 16, he was a logging crew foreman and a timber cruiser. During the 1840s, Stephenson moved to the Great Lakes and used his experience as a cruiser to buy timberlands in Michigan. Over the next 70 years, he built his own logging empire in the Lake States. He owned forests, steamboats, and sawmills.

Frederick Weyerhaeuser was an even bigger lumber baron than Stephenson. Weyerhaeuser was born in Germany in 1834 and moved to the United States when he was 18. He worked on a farm, at a beer brewery, and as a railroad laborer, before getting a job at an Illinois sawmill. Weyerhaeuser soon became manager of the mill, which was on the Mississippi River.

Wealthy lumber barons bought up forests all over the country

A KING'S MANSION

Lumber barons and kings had money to spend. They bought forests, railroads, and mining companies. They built boats, sawmills, and huge homes for their families, called mansions. One of the biggest of timber king mansions was built by lumberman William Carson. Carson's mansion in Eureka, California, was built of redwood from his own forests. Its 18 main rooms had carved wood archways, wall panels, and moldings. A 68-foot redwood tower faced his sawmill.

Frederick Weyerhaeuser

When the mill owners went broke, Weyerhaeuser used his savings to buy them out. He and his brother-in-law became business partners and bought other mills. But Weyerhaeuser wasn't satisfied with just buying logs and cutting them into lumber. He knew he could get logs more cheaply if he owned the logging companies that cut trees down.

Weyerhaeuser went to the Wisconsin pine forests and bought timberlands. Then he hired lumberjacks to cut, haul, and raft his logs to his own sawmills on the Mississippi River. Weyerhaeuser now owned a logging company, a rafting company, and sawmills. But he still wasn't satisfied.

Weyerhaeuser and other lumbermen on the Mississippi River competed for logs at the booms. Booms were like floating corrals that stopped logs and held them along the river at different sawmills. Lumbermen had to sort through log brands at each mill to pick out the logs they owned. This was done many times along the way, wasting time and money. Weyerhaeuser decided to improve the system.

He started an association for lumbermen called the Mississippi River Logging Company. The company organized tree cutting, and log hauling, rafting, and sawing. Trees were cut, moved, and sawed into lumber more quickly and cheaply. This was only the beginning for Weyerhaeuser.

Weyerhaeuser and other lumbermen like Orrin Ingram bought up timberlands in the Lake States, the South, and the West. They bought state and federal lands, and also lands owned by railroad companies. Weyerhaeuser came to be called the "Pine Land King." In time, he owned railroads, banks, and other businesses. By 1913, the Weyerhaeuser Timber Company was the largest in the nation.

Weyerhaeuser and others became lumber "barons" and "kings" as they built logging into an organized, national industry. They changed the way logging was done in the U.S. Small-time logging companies couldn't compete and had to sell out to the barons.

The growing lumber industry meant big business for saw companies

The Logger of Today

The modern logger almost never uses an ax or a handsaw. He doesn't ride down rivers on the backs of logs or skid logs with ox teams. His tools and methods have changed. But he still cuts down trees, hauls logs, and saws lumber. The logger of today still makes his living in America's forests.

Logging changed through the years of the 1800s and 1900s. Machine-age inventions like steam power made logging easier and quicker. By the 1920s, steam power was being replaced with a more modern invention—the gasoline engine. By the 1930s, gasoline-powered inventions were entering the timberlands.

The gasoline-powered chain saw put an end to the ax and handsaw. Chain saws are turned by a motor housed inside the saw. The motor spins a sharp-toothed chain that quickly cuts through wood. A logger working alone with a chain saw can cut down a six-foot-wide tree in two minutes. That's ten times faster than old-time loggers working in two-man teams with axes and handsaws.

The modern logger uses chain saws for felling trees, trimming off branches, and cutting logs. For loading and hauling, he uses other modern inventions, like the logging tractor. The logging tractor is also called a bulldozer. Loggers have their own name for these huge gas-powered vehicles. They call them "Cats," which is short for the Caterpillar company that makes them.

Logging tractors have made loggers into modern-day Paul Bunyans. Tractors run on ribbed treads called crawlers that grip the ground. The loggers who drive them are called cat-skinners. Tractors are powerful machines for skidding logs. Logs are tied to cables which are then hauled in by the tractor. Tractors are also used to clear ground for tree felling and for clearing logging roads.

Another gas-powered machine used by modern loggers is the tower skidder. Tower skidder cables are run from the top of a steel tower into the woods. A logger called the choke setter then hooks the cable to a log. Tower skidding is the modern version of high-lead logging. Logs are hauled through the air by the cable, then loaded onto trucks.

Modern lumberjack felling a Douglas fir in Oregon

A logger chains down a truckload of logs

LOGGING BY HELICOPTER AND BALLOON

In some areas, logging is done with giant helium balloons, blimps, or helicopters. In this way, loggers can handpick trees and avoid building roads. In balloon logging, cables hang from the floating balloon to the woods below. Logs are tied to a cable, then lifted by the balloon and guided to a loading area. Helicopter logging is useful in hard-to-reach areas of timberland. Helicopters lower cables into the woods where they are hooked to logs. The helicopter then flies off with its load.

Blimps haul logs out of hard-to-reach places

Cranes can lift dozens of logs at a time

Gas-powered logging trucks replaced logging railroads. Unlike railroads, logging trucks don't need tracks. They can go most anywhere in the woods where tractors have cleared logging roads. Trucks haul logs directly to sawmills.

Modern mills need few mill workers. Automatic conveyors, saws, planers, edgers, and sanders cut and finish lumber in record time. All of the machinery is controlled by computer.

The modern logger lives with his family close to the logging areas. He works either for big lumber companies or for himself. If he is a company employee, he works for a salary. If he works for himself, he is called a private contractor. He cuts and hauls with his own tractor and truck, then sells the logs.

Logging and the Environment

To the European settlers, North America's forests seemed to stretch on forever. A squirrel could go from Maine to Louisiana by jumping from one tree to the next, without ever touching the ground. That changed as European axmen cut down whole forests.

When Europeans first arrived in the Northeast, there were about 850 million acres of forests in North America—covering almost half the country. Over the next two hundred years, pioneer loggers cut down 100 million acres of trees—an area larger than Montana. Between 1850 and 1880, lumberjacks cleared another 100 million acres of forest. It was just the beginning.

New inventions helped loggers do the job quicker. By 1920, only 470 million acres remained of the original 850 million. Few people cared about the loss of so many trees. Wood and wood products were needed in America and around the world. Most people thought that the forests would last forever.

In the 1800s, some citizens and political leaders began talking about saving America's forests. They said that if logging continued at such a quick pace, there would someday be no forests left. They feared that the United States could wind up without timber like England and some other countries.

The loss of trees was just part of the problem. Trees are parts of ecosystems. An ecosystem is a living environment of soil, plants, water, and animals. Every part of an ecosystem is connected to the other parts.

A bare hillside marks the place where this forest was clear-cut

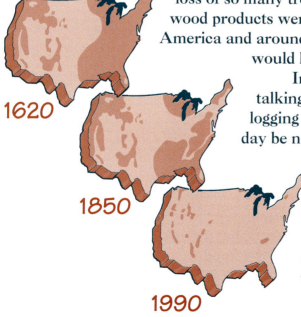

1620

1850

1990

The original hardwood forests of the United States have nearly vanished

42

For instance, birds and other animals make their homes in trees. Forests are called habitats, or places animals live. As trees are cut down, animals lose their habitats—and their lives. Some birds, such as spotted owls, depend on old-growth forests to survive. Old-growth forests were here when Europeans arrived in North America. Loggers cut most of them down.

The very last of the ancient old-growth forests remain in the West. Other U.S. forests are called second-growth. They grew in place of some forests that were logged out. However, scientists have found that old-growth forests support more wildlife than newer forests.

Old rotting trees are homes to insects, birds, and small animals. Old-growth forest soils are rich in nutrients for plant growth. Cutting down old forests is like tearing down homes and neighborhoods where people live.

Some animal groups, called species, are in danger of extinction as their habitats are destroyed. Extinction means the end of life for an entire animal group, like spotted owls. Other species, like bald eagles and peregrine falcons are in danger of extinction too.

People's lives also depend on trees. Trees need water, sunlight, and carbon dioxide which they get from the air. In a chemical process called photosynthesis, trees make the energy they need to live on. They also produce oxygen and release it into the air we breathe.

Chopping down old-growth forests leaves many animals homeless

Humans breathe in oxygen, use it to live, and then breathe out carbon dioxide. Oxygen and carbon dioxide, therefore, pass between people and trees. Without trees, we couldn't live and breathe.

Modern pulp and paper mills pollute the environment

By taking carbon dioxide from the air, trees also control the earth's temperature. As the sun warms the earth, some of the heat escapes back into space. However, too much carbon dioxide in the air blocks the heat from escaping. This is called the greenhouse effect. Without trees to use carbon dioxide, the earth will become too hot for human life.

Cutting down whole forests, or clear cutting, causes other problems too. As trees are logged out, soil is exposed. Rich forest soils are then washed away, or eroded, by wind and rain. Soil is washed down hillsides into rivers, clogging waterways and killing fish. Fertile land is lost and waterways are ruined.

Lumber and pulp mills also cause problems to the environment. Pulp mills grind wood into a paste to make paper and plastics. Giant mills pollute the air with wood dust, chemicals, and gases that cause lung disease.

Today, most of the original North American forests are gone. But some old woodlands now grow new trees. The U.S. government limits logging in the nation's forests. Loggers are no longer permitted to cut down every tree in sight.

SAVING AND GROWING TREES

Some modern lumber companies don't just cut down trees—they grow them. Tree farms are planted where old-growth forests once stood. As trees are harvested, new trees are planted in their place. Some people hope that with tree farms, wild forests will be left alone. Recycling is another way to save trees. Used paper, instead of trees, can be made into pulp for new paper. Another way to save trees is to make paper from tropical plants like hemp and kenaf.

The National Forest Service and some logging companies plant seedlings where old-growth forests once stood

INDEX

American Revolution, 7

axes, 6, 16, 18, 25

axhead—cutting edge of an ax, 18

ballads, 34-35

balloon logging, 41

Bangor Tigers—river drivers from Maine, named after the logging town of Bangor, 16

bedroll—blankets, 17, 20

bindle stiff—a term for a logger, because he was a wandering laborer (stiff) who carried his bedroll (bindle), 17

bindle—a logger's blankets, also called a bedroll, 17

birling—sport of logrolling, in which two lumberjacks stand on a floating log and turn it with their feet to see who can balance longer, 34

blimp logging, 41

boom—floating log fence that trapped floating logs in rivers alongside sawmills, 11, 39

Bradbury, Logger, 36

British navy, 7

buckers—loggers who trimmed off branches and cut trees into short logs, 17

buffalo range, 4

bummer cart—wagon used to drag cut logs out of the forest, 12

Bunyan, Paul, 34

California Gold Rush, 24

calk—pointed metal spike, 19

calked boots—boots with sharp metal spikes on the bottom that gave loggers sure footing on trees and floating logs, 19

camp cooks, 37

camps, logging, 9, 20-21

cant hook—a 5-foot-long wooden pole with a sharp hook at the end, used to load and unload logs, 9, 18-19

cant hook men—loggers who used cant hooks to pile logs along river banks for the log drive down river, 10, 18

caralog—bummer cart with 12-foot wheels, used to transport huge tree trunks, 23

Carson, William, 38

chain saw—a gasoline-powered tool whose engine spins a sharp-toothed chain that quickly cuts through wood, 40

choppers—loggers who cut down trees with handaxes, 17

choppings—timberlands where lumberjacks cut down trees, 21

chutes—troughs carved out of logs and laid end to end that carried logs down mountainsides by the force of gravity, 25

clear-cutting—cutting down whole forests without replanting, 44

clothing, lumberjack's, 19

company town, 22

crosscut saw, 25

ecosystem—living environment of soil, plants, water, and animals, 42

environmental damage, 42

Erie Canal, 15

erosion—process of soils being washed away by wind and rain after the protective layer of trees has been chopped down, 44

fallers—loggers who chopped down trees with axes, 9, 30

falling saw—narrow, thin saws used to cut down giant redwood trees, 18

falling—chopping down trees with handaxes (also called felling), 17

fire grass—young plants that sprouted after a fire had burned through an area, 3

flumes—chutes filled with water that carried logs downhill, 25

food, 21

forest fires, 4, 31

go-devil—simple sled on which logs were hauled out of the forest, 9

Gold Rush, 24

greenhouse effect—the effect of too much carbon dioxide in the air, which prevents heat from escaping the Earth's atmosphere, 44

helicopter logging, 41

Hodag—mythical forest creature with the face of a lion, horns of an ox, and the spiny back and tail of a dinosaur, 35

Hurd, Perley, 36

immigrant loggers, 16-17

Ingram, Orrin, 39

jammers—loggers who worked along river bends and shallows to prevent logs from piling up during a log drive, 10

Jones, Jigger, 37

kickback—the cut base of a tree skipping backwards on the stump, endangering lumberjacks, 30

log drive—process of transporting thousands of logs down river from the forest to the sawmill, 9

log jam—huge pile-ups of logs that blocked drives down river, 11

logger—worker who cuts down trees and sells the logs for a profit, 3, 8

logging camps, 9, 20-21

logging tractor—a gas-powered bulldozer that runs on ribbed treads that grip the ground, 40

lumber barons—wealthy lumbermen (also called timber kings) who owned forests and sawmills, 13, 22, 38-39

lumber towns—towns that were built around sawmills, usually next to a river, 32-33

lumber—wood that has been cut into boards, 2

lumberjack—professional logger who worked for logging company owners and were paid a monthly wage, 8-9, 10-12, 13, 15, 17, 18, 19, 20-21, 23, 24-25, 28, 30-31, 32-37, 40-41

lumbermen—logging businessmen who owned timberlands, trees, and sawmills, 3

modern logging, 40-41

Native Americans, 4-5

old-growth forests—forests that existed when the first Europeans arrived in North America, 43

peavey—long-handled pole with a hook and a spike on the end used to pull logs out of piles and push them into the river, 10, 18-19

photosynthesis—chemical process by which plants absorb sunlight, make the energy they need to live from it, and produce oxygen and release it into the air, 44

pull boat—flat-bottomed boat with a steam-powered engine mounted on top, used to haul logs from Southern swamps, 23

rafting—lashing logs together and floating them down river to sawmills, 14-15

railroads, 23

railroads, 23, 24, 26-27, 31

recycling, 43

rivermen—lumberjacks who rode on top of logs as they floated down river to sawmills, 9, 10, 30-31

road monkey—lumberjacks who watered roads at night so that log-carrying sleighs could slide easily over the frozen surface in the morning, 13

Ross, John, 36

sackers—lumberjacks who rode at the tail end of the log drive, prying loose stray logs that had become stranded on rocks, islands, and bushes, 10

sawmills, 7, 28-29

sawyer—sawmill worker who cut logs into lumber, beams, shingles, and other products, 28

scaler—logger whose job was to measure logs and brand each one to show which company it belonged to, 9

second-growth forest—forests that grow in place of some forests that have been cut down, 43

self-loader—steam-powered crane mounted on a railroad flatcar that transported logs onto railroad cars, 27

shanty—bunkhouse shack in a logging camp, 20

Silver Jack, legendary fighting logger, 34

skid road—road built from logs and covered with grease to help ox teams skid logs out of the forest, 25, 33

spotted owls, 43, 44

springboard—platform inserted into the trunk of a tree 10 or 12 feet above the ground, where the trunk was thinner and easier to cut through, 25

squatting—settling on land without paying for it, 6

Stephenson, Isaac, 38

Stewart, Jim—champion logroller, 34-35

swampers—loggers who built forest roads to haul logs on, 9

tall tales, 34-35

timber cruisers—men who scouted forests for lumber companies to select the best timberland, 12

timber—trees that are cut down and sold as logs or wood products, 2

timberlands—areas where pine and other useful lumber trees grow, 2

tree farms, 43

wangan—lumber company wagons that supplied lumberjacks with food, tools, and camping gear along the drive, 11

wedge—steel tool that lumberjacks jammed into sawcuts to keep the cuts open and allow saws to move freely, 18

Weyerhaeuser, Frederick, 12, 24, 38-39

whipsaw—saw with handles on both ends, 28